It Will

Rain

Just when you think everything is going well...
life happens but through the dry seasons,

It Will

Rain

Levia Gee

authorHOUSE®

AuthorHouse™ LLC
1663 Liberty Drive
Bloomington, IN 47403
www.authorhouse.com
Phone: 1-800-839-8640

THE HOLY BIBLE, NEW INTERNATIONAL VERSION®,
NIV® Copyright © 1973, 1978, 1984, 2011 by Biblica, Inc.®
Used by permission. All rights reserved worldwide.

Published by AuthorHouse   12/23/2013

ISBN: 978-1-4918-3063-5 (sc)
ISBN: 978-1-4918-3062-8 (e)

Library of Congress Control Number: 2013919431

About the Book

A HEART- FELT WARMING story of a young-African girl who is trying to make it in America; it is all about finding hope and courage to survive in the midst of life crisis.

Table of Contents

A Dedication . . .

I WOULD LIKE TO dedicate *It Will Rain* to a very special person; an ordinary girl who looks exactly like me. Last night the Lord granted me a vision. I saw her face and it was filled with tears.

The Lord showed me the great pain in her and I felt it too. I can hear her say "I'll never make it" She carries the weights of the world on her shoulder. She aims to live up to their expectations but she struggle every time and just doesn't make it through. She is too afraid to dream out loud. Well this is a new beginning and I'm telling her the worse is over. I've been on this very road she is taking now. I suggest you get your head straight; think positively! The flesh is weak but the spirit is strong. Lord I pray to please help her to know she's not alone. In the darkest hour there is hope at the end of the tunnel. Just keep walking and you'll reach the bright light at the end. Can you feel? There is a spark of light at the end.

About the Author

I AM AN ORDINARY girl with a burning desire to find comfort and happiness in life. I came from a small family of 4: I am sort of the middle child. I am originally from a small town of West Africa. I moved in the U.S with my mom at the age of 11. I went to elementary school for two years and then during my second year of middle school I was placed in foster care. Ever since than I've been tossed around from home to home and attended several different schools. I recently graduated from Colorado Springs Early Colleges and am now attending Pikes Peak Community College (ppcc). My hope is to get my associate at ppcc and transfer to CSU-Pueblo where I can Further my education and get my bachelor in social work.

I did not visualize my career as a social worker. But because of all the hurts and everything I've been through it made me a stronger and a better person. I want to help in the way I was helped. Social work is a great opportunity for me to give back to the community.

I personally believe the pain and hurts we experience don't last forever; tomorrow is always a new day and you'll see the sunshine. I don't know who you are; we haven't met before but believe me, you are my friend. As I sat on my desk and begin writing I pray for God to give me wisdom and understand so that I may bless you.

I can read your mind and I know what you're thinking. We are strangers. Yes I'm very aware of that. If you know well you probably know that family is important to me. I believe black or white, whether biological or adopted we are all created equal and love is what bonds us together. It helps us to get through the difficult time. My brothers, let me bless you with peace and grace as you read this book and begin a new journey.

Foreword

SOMEONE ONCE TOLD ME that a story is not a story if it is not shared and read by others. I believe this is true and that every story has its own uniqueness. When I wrote this short story my intention was to help people raise their spirits and find reasons to continue with their life; nevertheless, I too was encouraging and helping myself. I was grieving and finding healing as I sat there on a desk writing the story. We only have few chances to touch hearts in this life. Sometimes to make a difference, it requires us to make sacrifices; we have to get out of our comfort zone.

I am so grateful to Ms. Quinda, my caseworker who had been with me every step of the way. She was the most honest and loving person I've ever met. In my darkest hours she didn't baby me with encouraging and sweet words, rather tells me the hard truth, things I didn't want to hear. She went above and beyond her normal work. She was my hero and more like a mother to me.

Ms. Quinda, I love you more than words can describe.

I also want to honor my foster mom and the rest of the Lutheran Family Service staff.

Levia Gee

You guys are just amazing and incredible! I know I can be a little annoying and tough sometime but you guys dealt with me and never gave up on me. You guys helped me to release and relive certain experiences that I never wanted to remember. Now I've got a troop of army behind me.

Alright Santa, what you got for me in your next game? Well whatever it is, this time, I'm ready for you! I am stronger than before because I have God on my side; bring it on! I'm ready to play the game. Yeah I'm in it to win the battle.

Prologue

Me, to America? There is no way; they must be joking with me!

Somebody pinch me and wake me up! Maybe this is just a daydream, it is not possible.

All my life, I've never dreamed or even imagined of stepping my feet into America's land.

But the message was loud and clear. I was going to America!

The New Kid

THERE IS A NEW girl at Brooklyn High School. She and her family have just moved here this summer and she has transferred to this new school. This is the year she has hoped for a new balance, something new. Everybody is talking and wondering about her and she is so tired of always having to be the new student. Some students gazed at her intently as she enters the classroom. She smiles politely as she is walking to the back of the classroom. Then she spots an empty seat and she asks the teacher if it is taken; impressed by her warmness, the teacher looks at her and simply says "No." The other students turn and look at her with grinning faces but she can see the sadness and the hate behind their hazel eyes.

The "new kid" wanders off hopelessly. She was lost in the wilderness. Nobody knows her. She feels like a fool. She sits all alone and wait patiently; for a new friend to come along. She tries her best to stay strong and play it cool but every day was mostly the same. Nobody knows what she was going through. She puts on a smile and tries to fit in but nothing was working out right. Her heart is filled with despair and sorrow but there is nowhere to hide. Hello, my name is Levia and this is my story.

My very own Words

I am a girl
People criticize me all the time
Some say I complain a lot and
I always have a negative view on life
The truth is I like to suggest something or
Make a counter statement because this is the only way
I know how to let my voice be heard

I am a girl
People say mean things about me
But obviously they don't know anything about me
I just want to sing and dance to my favorite song
So that I can forget all about the gossips in the air

I am a girl
I'm eighteen years old
I've never had a boyfriend and I've never been kissed
I think to myself, I'm just a filthy, ugly girl
My family and friends, they all say I'm beautiful
But honestly, I believe they're only trying to be nice to me

I am a girl
I am sweet with a little bit of spicy on the side
There is a time when I'm fun and playful
There is also a time I get real serious

I am a girl
I can't quote the entire Bible
Sometimes I break the golden rule
I am just like everybody else
I fight with my family and friends
But I also have a great love for people

I am a girl.
I am a talented girl full of passion
I love to write poems and to sing;
Music inspires me to hope and dream
I have a strong desire to do something great for the world;
To shine the light and bring hope in people's lives.
But for now, I must set my head straight.

I am a God girl and that's all I'll ever be
My heart's desire and prayer is to be a servant of God
and live according to his gracious power.

My name is Levia. Well at least that's what everybody calls me. My friends and families know me as Levia; because that was what I told them. My name is rare, and uncommon. Almost everyone I know found it hard to pronounce. I can't blame them, some things just need practice.

Now you might ask "why?" Well, that is a great question!

To make things a little more sense let me take you to the beginning of the story.

I have a past. I have some secrets that are buried deep within my heart. This is where it all begins. This is where I find my fault; through the pain I when I feel hopeless and think there is no reasons for me to live, healing rain comes pouring down. Yes, it does rain. Just wait and see. This is what I learned.

Sometimes I scream, yell and act mean just to get attentions. Yes, I didn't know how to communicate properly and interact with the world around me. Most people are afraid and scared for my life. They say my behavior is intolerable. I am constantly being watched on a microscope. Every move I make, every steps I take must be approved by them, otherwise I'm not accepted into the world. This amazes me every time and I say to myself, "Wow! What a cruel world we live in."

When I walk into my room I can see a picture in a frame. This picture frame is sitting on my headboard. It is a picture of a young girl who looks exactly like me. She is wearing a white strapless dress with brown polka dots. For the jewelry part, she wears a . . .

Every time I enter the room she has a bright smile on her face. All the while, she stares right at me, looking straight into my face as if she is searching for an answer in the eyes of a stranger. Yeah, that girl in the picture frame is me. She used to be filled with love and laughter's. Before she used to enjoy life more than anyone could ever have imagined. But now she is totally a different person; a stranger to herself.

Sometimes I would pick up the picture, lie on my bed and hold the frame to my chest; just imagining and trying to listen to what she has to say. I know all too well that she is just a picture and will never speak to me, still I wonder and mumble to myself as if someone is listening.

Lord what happened to me? I wonder what went wrong in my life. My hopes and dreams, where did they all go? No responses. Only a dead silence is floating in the air.

I was a pure, innocent child from Africa. At the age of 1 I lived with both my Father and Mom along with my older sister. I thought everything was perfectly normal. Then suddenly the most despicable and horrific thing happen: a civic war break out in my small my village. A few months later, my Dad joined the army when I was still a year old. With the war going on and my mom being a single mom, things became very difficult for her. The quality of the relationship between my mom and my Dad was no longer the same. We often did not see my father because he was always deployed when he was in the military.

As if this was not enough both my parents got separated. There was no such as divorced because my mom was never married to my Father. This gave my Father an excuse to do the most unspeakable, disgusting thing. He abandoned his family and got a new girlfriend.

I was a child back than but few years down the road when my mom told me the story I felt like my whole world was crumbling down. Part of me wanted to believe that my father loved us but there were always doubts in her mind. My mom was having a difficulty times coping with this new change; for she too never once had imagined that one day she would be losing my Dad to another woman.

So she got involved to make the matters even more worst. She would say negative things about my Father to brainwash me and basically tries to stop me from ever thinking about my father. At this point, it really didn't matter to me. There were no other sources; I could only listen to her side of the story. I was only a child when we left. I don't remember anything about him.

I didn't know my father.

A few years down the road my mom decided to move the entire family to another country, to try to reboot her life. She moved my sister and me to Burkina Faso, located in West Africa. When my mom met another foreign man, she had two kids with him-both were boys. When my little brother was born, our mom decided to let my older sister and I go live with a relative. They send us off to Guinea, a country located in West Africa to live with the people we've never met before. Surprisingly we were happy to live there. My sister and I thought this was going to be a great opportunity for us to meet new family. We thought this was going to be a fun adventure! We head off to Guinea where two of his sisters live. I was so glad when my sister and I was a neighbor but my poor brother had to live couple blocks away from us. Even though our little brother was not living with us, it didn't bother my sister and I because we knew our brother didn't live far from us. We were told he can come visit us whenever he wants to and versa we go to his house anytime. My sister and I had a close relationship. When she cooks she call me and I too would bring my and we share a meal together. I went to her place and sleep there many times. We cry together and laugh together like sisters.

We lived with our Aunts from two years than our parent came back for us. They came with a cute, little boy. I glared at him and smile. I study his face; he looked nothing like my other brother. "Say hi girls. This is your little brother." She said. "Hi." I smiled. He sucked his thumb and turns his head toward mom. "Cool. Now I have two brothers and one sister." "Well, your father and I miss you guys so much and we think it's time to take you two home." So we packed our things and left Burka Faso, to go back home.

At home nothing was like it used to be. I knew there was something different between mom and her boyfriend. There were not close as they use to be. I thought things were fine between them. I thought they were happy. They would constantly argue and fight; then make up. It was like that and I was so disgusted and tire of both of them. I watched them fought verbally and sometimes physically. At one point it got extremely bad that I went in between them to try to break up the fight. My mom's boyfriend, supposedly my stepfather hit mother with a stick and he also ended up hitting me on the face. For the very first time, I saw tears pouring down my mother's face like a waterfall. She was in pain and my heart was broken. It wasn't a pleasant sight seeing my mother like this. She deserves better than this.

Finally it was as if she'd seen the light. She packed her things and decided to leave him for good. Lucky for my brothers, they didn't get to see all the drama; for they were still with his relative back in Guinea. I was completely lost and confused. It was like being shock by electricity. Blood was flowing through my veins and my heart was pounding violently as I watched my mother walks away. I was of an emotional, dramatic person but my sister; she was more of a clam, peaceful person. My mom used tease to and tells my sister she was the dumb one in the family because most of the time she was quiet and doesn't pay attention to things around her. She stood there in the door way, frozen like a status. She didn't want to leave. "Come on." My mom grabbed her hand. This is goodbye; I hope to never see your face again!" She cried out her boyfriend. These were her final words to the man whom she never married.

I was sad and terrified; I didn't want to leave the place, everything I knew. But I just couldn't watch my mother leave alone. It was very difficult because I had to choose between two parents. I chose my mother and my sister too followed us. Now we left Burkina Faso and went back to Liberia; where we originally came from. But, as always nothing had changed. My mom left me in the village and then went back to the city. Once again, I was left in Grand Gedeh, Liberia to live with a distant relative. I thought this was only a temporary thing. I thought I would be separated for a short amount of time. But I waited, and waited. There were times I even thought she had forgotten about me.

There I waited patiently. Days turned into weeks, weeks into months and months in a year. I finally heard from her but it was not the way I have imagined.

A huge change and an opportunity came in my life when I was nine and just about getting ready to turn ten.

It was late midnight and I've already gone to bed and had fallen asleep. One of my host families came in the room to wake me up. I gazed at her, scared and confused, rubbing my eyes and still waking from a sleep. It was obvious that she could see the concern and the anxiety in my eyes because she said "Don't be afraid or dismayed my child, you are not in trouble." There is someone who wants to meet you." She continued. She me told there was a lady waiting for me outside. I slowly opened my eyes and stumbled out the room to meet this mystery person. The woman looked at me with admiringly eyes and smiled politely as she shakes my hand. Then she asked what my name was. I stared at her face trying to make sense of what was going on. I grabbed a chair and sat next to her. It was too dark and I couldn't see her face clearly. It wasn't until the next morning that I was able to see every detail of her face.

She was a woman in her 40s. She has light skin and I thought she was from somewhere out of town. As I stared at her, I noticed one of her eyes was squinted. I was nervous and scared of the stranger. I also felt sad and sorry for her and wonder what happened to her eye, but I quickly stopped myself from asking her that question. It was rude and means to stare at a person, so I keep turning my head look the other way. Whenever I speak, I look over her shoulders to avoid looking at her face.

The woman told me my mother was in Ivory Coast and is living in a small house by herself. She than continue to say that my was very sick and wanted me to come before anything happens to her. A side from that I also received some good news. I was told that since my mother since was without home, she was considered a refugee and there is a very high chance that she might come to America.

9

However, because of her illness she wanted my sister and I to come take care of her. This was her mission: My mother had sent for me.

I've been on my own most of my life. There has been no one, ever. Nobody knows I even exist; except the almighty God, in whom I put my trust in. It really try to make it and only wish what my life would be better.

Just a Dream

I woke up screaming from a terrible dream. I do not know who were in the dream or what the dream was about. All I know is that it was sad and scary. My body was covered with cold sweat. I lay awake now, trembling with fears; all alone in the dark. I sat up on my bed and dazed at the radio. The crystal blue light shone right through my eyes. It was only the middle of the night; One o'clock to be exact. My little brown eyes turned red. I rubbed one eye and then the other in the most uncomfortable way and instantly tears started dripping down my cheeks. I was surrounded by darkness. I needed someone to be there and tell me I was loved and everything would be alright. But as I turned on the light everything became clear. I was just a small town girl who in need of compassion, the kind of love that's never failing. In the midst of this thoughts were flowing in my mind and my soul became restless. I was reaching out to someone but only silence is in the air. Heaven hear me now, for I'm trembling from my past.

The "American Dream"

I was told in one of my class Mount Everest is one of the highest mountains in the world. They says it stretches along the border of Nepal and Tibet and goes through China in southern Asia. Because of its great height Mount Everest is said to be the most dangerous mountain in the world. Despite this, many people still climb it to experience the adventure of a lifetime; whether it means death. Several people have lost their lives trying to climb this tremendous mountain and gaining the title of heroism. We all know that accomplishing anything in life requires a great deal of devotion and effort.

Sometimes I close my eyes and imagine that climbing Mount Everest is the same as coming to America. Although they are different concepts I believe they are relatively alike. Yes, it is. Many people risk their lives to come to America.

The United States is said be known as one of the leading country for immigrants. It is among many other countries that generally welcome immigrants' people. All different types of people from all over the world come here with dreams and hopes of the ultimate "promised land". Many people move for a variety of reasons; however they all have one thing in common: they want to achieve the "American Dream".

"The American Dream" is a profound idea that has been pondered in our heads and also has made the U.S an attractive destination for many foreigners countries. Many people believe a person can achieve a "successful, richer and happier" life if they work really hard and have a solid, clear vision. Some of the practical reasons many risked their lives to venture out in America is because that they can seek political, religious freedom, and economic opportunity, and the educational privileges, as well as to build a better lives. Yes and yes, I was among many of the millions of people that immigrated to the U.S to pursue the "American Dream," so to speak. It seems like just a couple of years ago my mother and I came here. My mom and I came to the U.S when I was 11 years old. As recall I some of these memories, it seems like just a couple of years ago that my mom and I immigrated to America. I came here with high dreams and expectations for my life. I didn't know or had forgotten all about the long road I would have to take and the high mountains I would have to climb to get there. I had imagined America as this magical place, almost like Heaven. I originally thought life would be better life when I come to America. I thought my prayers had finally been answered. Sure, America is a dream and a land of opportunity. Most people are desperate to come here to America. My dreams and hopes were set pretty high. I thought I would graduate from college; get a good job, a house and a car. I also wanted to start a family. Yes, these were the dreams and hopes, as well as my own imaginations. But as it turned out, they were all just a dream. I found myself being hit in the face with reality.

Let's be honest, achieving the "American Dream" was much more difficult than anyone could ever imagined.

Though I cannot deny the fact that coming to America was a great opportunity; it was something to ask for, something to dance for but I can't help to stress the fact that sometimes I feel like coming to America has been a blessing and a curse. I use to think that we were the lucky ones to come to America. I mean coming here was like winning a lottery ticket. It is extremely hard for people to enter into the U.S. Yes. It was the magical thing that has ever happened to me and the happiest day of my life. It's like I was looking through a telescope and I can see where I was going; I was heading to America.

I do not know nor remember much about my childhood but one for certain was that I had a rough life growing up as a child. My mom did try to take care of me but she struggled most of the times. I had a single parent and so my whole life mostly revolves around moving from one place to another. I've live with many relatives and friends. But back then, I didn't think any of it less. Growing up as a child, I thought my country was the "best thing in the world." In fact I thought I my life in Africa was normal. My family was not poor, and myself; I had never experienced the hunger not until now that I realize I lost most of my childhood. A lot of time, it was like a contrivance puzzle. I made an effort to piece them together from the scraps of memories.

A Desperate Measure

WHEN WE FIRST CAME to the U.S. my mom and I were very happy. At first, everything was almost magical and things were going perfectly fine. I can't deny that things were very difficult at first. After we arrived about a month later I was enrolled in elementary school.

On my first day of school, my caseworker took me there. He went to the attendance office and talked to the administrator. The next thing I know he took me to my classroom. I notice a woman writing on the board which I presume to be the teacher. She smiled brightly at me as I entered the classroom and I took a seat in the front.

I watched my caseworker and the teacher as they exchanged their conversation. The woman did not look older than somewhere around 30 something years old. She was probably a mix of Hispanic and white. Her hair was neatly combed and pulled back. She also had a hair bow tossed to the front of her hair.

When I looked around I was surrounded by strangers; the majority of my classmates were White. Nobody knew me and I spoke very little English and therefore I was terrified to speak or say anything to anyone at the school. This also made it difficult for me to make friends.

"Ok, Levia. I have to leave now. Will you be ok?" Say my caseworker. I nodded my head slowly as to tell him I understood.

Shortly, she walks toward me. I stared at her with frighten eyes. I was feeling intense and my lips could not move. Then she asked me again. "What's your name sweetie?" "Levia." I responded quickly. "Oh, do you mean, O'livia.?" I was beginning to feel frustrated and annoyed by the teacher. "No, Ma'am." I said. "It is Levia. There is no O." "Oh wow! That is such a unique, beautiful name." "Thank you, Ma'am." I mumbled.

"Well, welcome. We are very glad to have you here, in our class." Then she walked to the front of the class

"Okay class, please settle down. Today, we have a new student in our class. She is from Africa! Isn't that's wonderful?" Now I want you all to please try to make her feel welcome. Ok?" Yes Mrs. Miller." The students responded in a chores voice.

I took a seat in the back of class and sat down. When I looked around I was surrounded by completely strangers; the majority of my classmates were White. Nobody knew me and I spoke very little English and therefore I was terrified to speak or say anything to anyone at the school. During the first few weeks, I felt like a status who can't find the words to speak. This also made it difficult for me to make friends. I was intimidated by this situation. I felt like a complete idiot. I look around and thought to myself, what am I doing sitting here with all these people? My intellect does not compare to them. They are probably mocking and talking bad about me under their breaths. These White folks went to school several years before me. They are more educated and smarter than me. These were the assumptions I was making and the reputation I was building for myself. Such a sad, sad feeling.

My mom working busing tables in a restaurant. Even though she had a job and was working, there was not enough money to support both of us. She was making about seven dollars an hour, which was basically a minimum wage. Though she never told me about how much she was making, I quickly figure it out. I thought I was on my way to achieving the "American Dream."

During the first half year of our arrival we had a lot of helps and supports. They provided Well were not completely on our own but we had a limited amount of resources. The matter got even worse when my mom lost her job and she couldn't keep up with the rent. We were also on welfare because had a low income.

Yes, we found our self relying more on the U.S government.

After my mom lost her job, and the apartment we became homeless and there was nowhere for us to go. We had no relatives or family to stay with and so life became very difficult. Fortunately, there were other refugees that were here before us and my mom became good friends with them. Those people took us in. They allowed us to stay with them while we I was going to school. This would also give my mom the opportunity to get a job and get back on her feet. As grateful I was I did not like the life style we were living in. A single mom with young child, how can one ignore this situation? I wanted a stable home. A place I could call home and aa quiet place I can come to after school, to study and do homework.

Unfortunately, sharing bedroom with my mom and sleeping on couch was not the best thing in the world. Also moving from place to place; staying with so called friends and relatives became such a bad habit for my mom that she sometime stopped searching for a job, and an apartment. There were times I felt like not coming home. On most days, I stay at school for tutoring and stuff and I would come home late, like around 6:00pm. Yes, I would get off the bus late and walking home alone myself at night. It was a scary situation and kind of sad but I felt more comfortable and safer at school and I just didn't want to come home.

It was just a matter of time after about a year that we both changed. We were constantly fighting. My relationship with my mom drastically changed and it was nothing like I've imagined. There were a lot of tensions between us. I lost respect for my mother.

Little by little, the school began to notice my situation. They begin to question me about my living situation. Of course I try to keep my life quiet and not let anybody know what was going on. I would tell my teachers and principle that I live with my mom and she takes good care of.

One day, I came home from school and my mom told me all about her day. She said she had went earlier to the African Market which use to located on Hancock and that she had met someone. She said there was a white lady who was willing to help us. She told me that this person took her to apply for food stamp and that the next week she was going to help her search for a job and maybe even get an apartment. I was as thrilled as can be and thought maybe things are going to get better. But first I had doubts and wanted to know more who this friends of hers was. So I than asked cautiously, "What is this lady name?" "Delicia" She answer. Then I processed to my next question. "Is she Black or White" "White." She answers quickly. "Look, you need to stop asking so many questions and just go with the flow. Trust me, she said she is going to help and we just need to accept it. I am the parent and I'm trying to do the best I can so beat it." "Mom, please there is no need to be angry with me. I was only trying to get a better understand of this situation. I just didn't want to give my hopes up, that's all." A week later she told me things were not going the way we had anticipated. She said her friend; the one we were staying with wanted us to start paying rent or look for a place of our own. So my mom decided to send off with the lady, "Delicia." as a temporary home until she figure out what to do. When all of this happened I had no idea. It was a completely shocked. I've never met this woman before, whatsoever. I mean Ms. Delicia came to my school. I had no idea how she knew where I was and how to find me. Obviously my mom must have told her, right? But no, it wasn't my mom. My mom only knew the name of the school and not even the address. Later, I learned that Ms. Julie had called the school and spoke to the principle. Though, it was a challenging task, she somehow mentioned to get my information, including my name, and the location of my school. If I remember correctly, I think it was during third week of February, in 2007. I remember Ms. Delicia picked me up from school, she took me to AFW restaurant and got something to eat. It was late, probably around 7:00pm when we went to her house and I was introduced to the rest of the family. At that time I didn't get a chance to stop at the old apartment to get my stuff. So she took to Target to do some clothes shopping. I will never forget this moment because I had drank a large cup of Pepsi earlier which caused me to have diarrhea. As remember this moment, it is also funny because it was the first time I got my first paired of bras.

The next day, we went back to my mom to try to get some of my stuff, miraculously my suitcase had already being packed and so all I needed was just grabbed it and leave. However, after we came out with the suitcase and was making my way towards the car, she suddenly had a mood of reaction. She said, "stop! Come back here with the suitcase." I turned to Ms. Delicia, she too turned and we both stared at each for a split second. "I'm sorry what?" She doesn't want me to go back with you?" I said back to her. "May I ask why? What's the matter?" "Don't take my daughter away from me!" She said firmly. "Mom, weren't you the one who suggested the whole thing and made the arrangement?" I need some of my stuff, especially my clothes and shoes. I them for school." But she has already made up her mind. She stood in front my suitcase and I was between her and Ms. Delicia. I try to convince her to let me go but the words of my plead flew right over her head; she was not listening to a word I was saying. It was than Ms. Delicia realized that it was going to be very difficult to talk to my mom and win so she told me to just get in the car. "Levia, your mom is very emotional right now and I don't think I should leave you here tonight. Let's just leave and give her some space. She needs some time alone to cool down. We can always plan to come again to get your stuff." And so I did. "I'm leaving mom. I will see you soon." I got in the car and we drove away. At that time I had nothing in mind. I thought it was a friend helping another person. But as it this was one radical moment, a decision that would change my life forever.

Two days later after the weekend I heard that my mom have moved once again, to a new place and is staying with a friend. I decided to go visit this new place and to see how she was doing. I told Julie to let me stay over. And there begins the longest night of myself. I, to be lecture from my mom, and her so-called friends. I sat there on the couch. I wasn't going to argue with the elders and throw a fit. They were saying all kinds of mean and horrific things about me. I've try to ignore everything but what hurts the most was when she told me I was an ignorant child. I do not act like her own children. The next thing said was that she didn't understand why I was short in structure and don't look anything like the rest of her children. It was then that I realize that my mom loves to bring me down. She knows very how to destroy me emotionally.

I sat on the coach stared at the window. There was nothing I could do or say. I sat alone, weeping and crying as if someone has passed away. She said, "Dry those tears off of your stupid face and stop your crying." I said, "Leave me along and just let me be." "You know what? That is it. I am not going to let you go to school tomorrow!" She snaps. "What!? You've got to be kidding me right me?" I snapped back. "No way! You can't do that. You have to let me go to school."

I snapped back.

"Watch me. You think I can't do that?" You are grounded for the rest of the week! I will lock you up in the room and you will not step your foot outside to see another light of the day."

Ok, obviously we were speaking in our native language but I kind of imagined it went something like that.

At first I didn't want to believe her but it was all real. The next day, I got up, brush my teeth, took a quick wash up and got dressed. As I turned the knob and was about to open the door, she knocked my bag out of my hands. She stood on the door and said, "Did you think I was joking when I told you weren't going anywhere?" So I turned around and sat back on the couch. Within the couples of hours, there was a knock at the door. My mom opened it, turned her heads to me and said, "Don't move. Stay right where you are." I don't know how or why but Department of Human Services showed up. She said, "Is Levia here." As soon I heard my name, I got up and walked towards the front door. I said, "Yes. I'm Levia." "Oh nice to meet you, Levia." "Is this lady your mom?" "Yes" I answered. "What's her name?" she asked. "Alice." Well, I heard that your mom doesn't speak English very well but I will try my very best." Ok. I said. Do you mind stepping outside for a quick moment?" "Mom, she wants you outside." So they went but I decided to follow them. Before I could go any farther, my mom yelled. "Go back inside! Don't you dare come out here!" But I refused. I decided to go against her. She came and started pushing me. D.S.H told my mom. Please stop, Ms. Alice." But my mom would not listen. I was walking and she kept pushing to go inside. The D.S.H became real nervous and began to call the police for help. The next thing I know, two police officers showed up. One of them interviewed and asked me many questions. I just didn't know what to say or what to do. I was scared and terrified at the police officer. "Well, here is the thing. Your mom wouldn't let you go to school but she can't do that. She has to let you go to school. Another thing is this isn't the best or safe environment for you. It looks like your mom is out of it right and I don't know if it is best to leave here tonight. Let me talked to the lady and see what says." "Yes, sir." As he left me alone. My mom started screaming and saying stuff. The officer said. "Ma'am, we're going to take your daughter away for a few hours and bring her back home. "No!" She blows it out. "Ma'am, your daughter will be gone for only a short amount of time. She will be with this lady. As I was being carry away, My mom suddenly dropped on the floor. She grabbed my feet and started crying. "Please, don't go. Stay here with me." Her other friend joined in and they both my feet. My mom was holding foot and the woman was holding the other. "Ma'am, I need you to let go of her." But all they were doing was crying and screaming. They officer put a handcuffs on my mom and she finally let go. "Please officer, don't arrest my mom." "I won't. I just needed her to stay calm." Shortly the officer took me to the car.

And there it was. At the age of 12 I got taken away from my mom.

The day I was taken away from my mom was the most horrifying experienced I've ever had. I still remember this moment as if it happened yesterday. It feels like a cold chill running down my soul. Lord only knows when I will ever get over this moment. I just want to feel safe and be ok again.

I see my whole world crush down before me as I was being pulled away by the social worker. I looked through the window and saw my mom sating on the floor. She was handcuffed like a criminal, tears were pouring down her face. Besides being at a funeral, this was the most I'd seen my mom cry.

I was taken to the Department of Human Service (D.H.S) office. I sat there quietly.

I watched the woman filled out paper works and asked me more questions. She than give me a bottle of water, some fruit snacks and a book called *My New Home.* "Before I catch you up on the plan, let me ask you one thing."

"Do you know Ms. Delicia?" "Yes ma'am. It does sound familiar." "Well, since you've already met her and have been to her house I figure it would be best to put you back with her." "Is that aright with you? Does that sound like a plan?" I nod my head in agreement. "Well, she will be here shortly to pick you up. Ok? "Ok." I answered.

This short planed turned out to be a long one. A day with Ms. Delicia, became a week and a month turned into a year; all because my mom refused to follow through with the court order. Yes, this was the starting point of my life.

After I moved with Ms. Delicia, next day I went back to school. I went back to because I had no choice; I was forced to go to school. I went back to school because I was told education was good for them mind, body and soul; it makes you much smarter. I went back to school but what good did do it for me? I was at a lost state and my mind couldn't focus. I sat in the classroom. I smiled and nod when the teacher looks at me but my mind was wondering elsewhere.

Soon I decided I didn't want to deal with her anymore. Part of me wanted to believe that my mom loved me but there were so many doubts in my mind. I wanted to believe and know that I was loved but what made it really hard and breaks my heart was that her actions were saying something completely different.

I gained some unique experiences when I was in the first foster home. Ms. Delicia, had already adapted two children from Africa so she knew what I was going. Many times, she try to play the role of mother and change my life around. One of the craziest things that happened was going shopping with Ms. Delicia. We went to Target which was a big deal for me because it was the real store I'd ever shopped at since I've been in America. Usually people from the church gave me clothes, which also helped my mom safe some money.

My mom and I usually shops at second-hand store such as Goodwill and the Arc. One time as I can recall, my mom and I went to the store, there was a woman who came from behind and started engaging a conversation with me. The next thing I know, she offered to buy me clothes. Of course it was free stuff on my part, so how can I say refuse? With my face flashing red, I simply smiled and said "Thank you."

One time, Ms. Delicia decided to do my hair. I knew very well, she probably had no idea how to do hair, especially African-American, but I said yes. Now why did I agree to let her do my hair? I'm not sure the answer to that but I think it was probably because I didn't want to offend her or act mean in any kind of way so I let her do it. We went to Wal-Mart and she asked me what I needed for my hair; I told her a relaxer and some hair grease. When we went to the aisle, there were so many hair products. "I'm not familiar with any of these ones but I think the *Beauty and Soft* might work. We came home, after she did it my hair was dry and frizzy. Many other likes also happened, like when she turned on the shower and I screamed. Also like the time I was force to eat cereal and pizza. Yes, those were some of the hilarious moment!

Than one day I was suddenly told that I have to move to another home. I asked her why, she never really explained it but the only excused I got was my caseworker told to her I have to move. Ms. Delicia had previously adopted two children from West Africa and she also have two biological kids of her own; Yes she had her hands full. I was the oldest one and the only teenage of the house. My caseworker said there were too many kids in the house and they won't be able to provide all the love and support I need. Financially, they can't take care of me. As hard and painful it was, they have to let me go, I was forced to move.

She said that there were too many kids in house and that her hand was full. "What do you mean? Am I too much trouble?" I cried out. "No, that's not it." "Than what is it!?" "Levia, I'm sorry. Please understand. I want you to know that I love you. I don't want to let you go but I was told that you needed a better home and as much as it hurts, I agree with them. You see, you are a teen and there is a lot you need and I feel like I'm not able to meet all your needs. For example, I can't take you to a beauty salon to get your hair or take you for clothes shopping because I can't afford to do that." Suddenly, I begin to think maybe she is right. I was the first teen she ever has and I'm growing and getting older each and every year. There were going to be a lot of things I need. First, I share room with two other kids. One girl was 5 and the other one was 3. It was difficult sharing room with them but I didn't mind.

I was told there were two families that were interested in me. And that I was going to spend time with each one of them, such as going out for lunch and doing activities with them. When I feel comfortable enough, I could possibly spend a night with them. I was sad but at the same time I was thrilled because I didn't have one but two people that wanted me in their homes and be part of their family. I visited them and every time I come home, I would tell Ms. Delicia all about fun adventures. Finally, it was time for me choose. I felt like a traitor or something. They each had a different home and unique family. I didn't want to break one either one of their hearts. I had to choose. It was time to decide. "So which families do you like better?" Ms. Delicia asked one time. I'm not quite sure but I think I like the Russo family." "Really? Would you mind telling me why?." "Well, I think the Russo family because the woman only has four sons and all of them are grown and only one still lives in the house. I don't think that'll be too much trouble because I don't like too many people around me." "Yes, I agreed with you too." I think she's the perfect choice because you'll be the only girl, as well as the youngest one at the house; she'll be able to focus more on you and give you all the attentions and love you need." "Remember, just because you're leaving doesn't mean you're gone forever and that we won't see each other. You have my number. You can call me whenever you want. I will still come to visit and spend time with you." I wrapped my arms around her waist and give her a hug. I smile at her. "I love you too."

On my last day Ms. Delicia asked me what I wanted to eat. "I don't know. Do we have enough money?" "Don't worry about it out right now. I want you to choose what you want to eat." "I don't know. What if everybody else doesn't like the food?" "Levia, this is all about you. I think they will pretty much eat anything." "Ok, well. How about some Chinese food?" So we order a whole bunch of Chinese food, invited some family and friends. After we ate, we took some pictures. It was a happy party. Everybody enjoyed themselves and I was very happy to see everyone there.

Since then, I've been in four different foster homes. Each time I've moved, I gained some unique and amazing experiences. I've been in so many places and lived so many homes but one of the craziest, miraculous things that happened to me was when I was in the second home. This second home was the Russo's.

Why, yes it was December; the most exciting time of the year! Christmas was around the corner. All scholar students were getting ready to get out of school for this special holiday break. Parents were stress out and going crazy about all the shopping they have to do. They joy of spending time and eating delicious meals with friends and family was all the reason to look forward for Christmas.

December, the end of the first semester and almost halfway through the school year. Usually, around the second weeks of December, students are getting to take finals. Oh yes, Lord knows I remember December, 2007. I've just moved to a new foster home and lived with the Russo family for about 4 months. I'd also just started eight grade at Discovery Canyon Campus.

I love December, that spectacular time month of the year. I look toward to this time of year because it is usually the radical period when people blossom and show the beauty and the love they have inside. Mrs. Russo had bought me a special outfit for me to wear to church on Christmas Eve. to go see the theatrical production of Life New, Wonderland. I was pretty excited and looking forward to Christmas Eve. Usually Mrs. Russo would get up early and make huge, delicious breakfast like pancakes, bacons and eggs. I always look forward to her cooking because she is a great cook and surprises us with different meals. However, December 9, 2007 she did not wake up early enough to make breakfast. I decided to surprise her with eggs and attempt to dry one of her pancakes recipes. After breakfast everyone scattered to get ready for church. Then we went to church like any other normal Sundays. Pastor Brady has prepared a surprise for New Life on that particular Sunday morning. He says he would not be speaking and that there was special guest, name Dr. Hayford and he couldn't wait to introduce him to the church. Dr. Hayford takes the stage and brought a strong, meaningful message to the congregation.

It was around noon the sermon was over; we head out the door. But somewhere, somehow my foster mom and I decided to stop by the front desk and visit some friends. This was what supposed to be a quick chat turned into a long conversation. I was standing there listening to my foster mom and her friend having their conversations. I stood there, glancing and smiling, appearing interested and it seem though as I was a big fan of what was going on but was bored as can be. Suddenly there was a crack of a sound which first appeared to have sounded like someone had popped a balloon or a firework. I told my foster mom. "It is probably nothing. I think some kid might be playing with a balloon or something. Than we heard the sound the second time again. "No, I think there is something. It smells like gun powder. Just a split second, before she can even finish her thought someone came running down the hall, yelling as loud as he could, "Get down! There is a shooting!" It was too late. We saw the man enters the building and coming toward us but he did not get any closer to us. Somehow, by the grace of God he went up stair to the children's ministry section. I will never forget the stunting look on my foster mom's face. She grabbed my hand quickly and we run out the door. There was a little girl, probably around 5 or 7 running around and crying for her parents. "Mommy, Daddy!"

Mrs. Russo was like "Come on Sweetie. Let's go find your parents. And so she grabs the little girl's hand and we ran to the next building. We were directed a room, where there were already people. The whole atmosphere was nothing like I'd imagined. The room was crowded with people. Husbands, wives and children, and family all crowed together, crying and praying. I asked her, "Where is Uncle?" "I don't know. Lord, please find my husband and keep him safe." We prayed, cried, prayed, cried that was all we did in the next 3 to 5 hours we were locked down. There was praise and worship, as well as prayers.

The funny thing is I felt the spirit of the Lord hovered over me. I was numbed and emotionless. I watch the entire congregation pouring with tears and praying but for some reason I was at peace. I knew God was among us, though we couldn't hear or feel him, he was not dead. We have been on lockdown for few hours pass noon. Usually I eat immediately after church when we get home, but was not able to eat on this particular Sunday. Lord I was hungry. All I could think of was food. I would be so happy if I just get something in my stomach. Not to make any excuses but what could one expect from a little girl? I was a small child back than. A little girl with dream and hopes. I had a lot of future ahead of me. No, I was not ready to leave this world. God knew there was something more for me; he had it all planned out. I know this for a fact. God's own words tells us in Jeremiah 29:11 I believe his words and z I hold them dearly in my heart. He didn't want to cut my life short. By the grace of God his tender love I was kept a live and given another to this life. It this wasn't a miracle I don't know what else to call it; It was indeed a miracle.

A few days later the shooter was identity. We learned that he was a 24-year-old white male named Matthew J. Murray

In the after math of the massacre some people were injured; leaving two young beautiful girls dead. Over hundreds of people our neighbors, friends and family were divested. Lord how can you let something like this happen? These were your precious daughters.

A year later, after this tragic event took place we went to church like usual. But I'd completely had forgotten that it was the anniversary of the shooting until the pastor brought it up. Those two teens who had lost their lives, they had left their family and friends with a horrific pain that will forever healed. It wasn't until that pastor Brady told the New Lifers to bowl their heads an take a moment of silent. Suddenly, as I lift up my head and take a look around, I saw the two girls as they were being show on the power point presentations. I was reminded that I had a blessing life. December 9, 2007 will not define my life or affect my future. 2007 could have been my last year living on earth but the Lord knew I wasn't ready; it was not my time yet to go. I was meant to be alive. But then the question rises, how could I had forgotten such an incredible moment?

I realized that I hadn't completely healed from the pain and that I was in denial. I try to forget about what happened a year ago and reincorporate my life but I have to deal with my pain and suffering before I can move forward. I turned around and knelt down at my seat. I prayed for healing and for the Lord to show me a new breathe of life. To learned to forgive and love those who had hurt me and trying to miss me up. At that moment I was at eased.

It was December, 2008 going on 2009. I have made it through those two years. I thought what could possible go wrong? Then suddenly Mrs. Russo brought her niece from New York. When I said New York, that girl was a New Yorker. She was talkative, curses a lot and just had a terrible attitude. But her Aunt wasn't letting this happened at her home. She quickly worked with her. Within the next two months, she made her changed her attitudes and that girl was a more respectful than ever. It was a total makeover. Her son, the one that was living at the house loves to tease and wrestle with her a lot. I didn't mind. Sometimes I would laugh and enjoy in but there were times he go overboard and it scares me. When the girl, she girls mad, she would scream and curse. Then she would slum the door. This I was not comfortable with me. One day, when the foster was at work, this happened. I told her and she talked to her son but he denied it. She didn't believe me and so our relationship begins to fall apart. So once again I had to move. First I had to meet and speak with them. During the first meeting, I learned Dad was a preacher. I freaked out and got a little nervous because as a preacher, I thought he would be more strike and harder on me. But I was wrong. I ended up having a great relationship and loving them.

It was Nov. of 2009 when I was placed in a new foster home. This new home was with the Jackson's family. They had one biological daughter and they also adopted two other children; one boy and one girl. When I moved there I really didn't have any problem with the family. I mean everything wasn't perfect but that's normal. There's going to be problem in any family.

One of the things that made it easier and helped me to adjust well was that fact they were Christian and they had a passionate heart for God. On most Sundays, we don't get much rest. We lived few miles away from the city and so we had to leave the house like around 8 in the morning to get to the church. Because we lived far out in the country, week days were even worst. We had to get up every morning at five. We have a family prayer and then we all get ready to leave for school at 6:30. Can't say I loved it. As matter of fact I hated it. There were time s I didn't want to get up at all. Nevertheless I was amazed at the way everybody forced themselves to get up I early in the morning and pull it all together.

Shortly after summer was over, I started high school. High school was a big deal. I felt like a mature, grown person. I was thrilled to set up all my classes and met new teachers.

When I first came to the U.S I was tiny and small. I remember when I was in 7th grade one day in my P.E class the teacher decided to take the students' weight and measurement so that we can get our uniforms. "Next!" I walked slowly toward the teacher. "What is your name?" She asked. I smiled and said "Levia." "Ok, Levia. Please step up on the scale." "Do you know by any chance how much you weight?" "No ma'am, I don't. I gazed at her. I could see a look, a concerned behind her big, blue eyes. "Well, let see. We'll find out in a minute. "Wow, you really are a tiny thing." She said jokingly. "Yes ma'am. I know." Then it hit me. Did she call me a "thing"? A "thing" sounded offensive and harsh. I am a girl, a human being. Why did she fail to recognize that? I remember feeling sad and frustrated but I manage to smile at her.

"Your weight is about 80." "Eighty. Thanks" I mumble. Compare to my other classmates eighty was such a small number. It was big deal. This number was a problem. I felt so tiny and out of place. I felt dead; like a plastic bag drifting through the wind. Just when I thought things could not get any worst, boy was I wrong. High school came. I was a freshman at Cheyenne Mountain. Sure I gain a little bit of weight and got taller but that they didn't help. I was small for my age and was always a year older than most of the other students. I always felt embarrass and ashamed of my body. I was in place of brokenness and hurting deeply inside. Every day, when I go out, whether it is the school, mall and even at the church I would always look around me. I see mostly tall girls with blonde hair; holding hands with their boyfriends. I begin to remember one of the songs from a Disney movie, Mulan. For some reason, "Reflection" came into my mind and I found myself singing it. *Look at me. I will never pass for a perfect bride, or a perfect daughter. Can it be I'm not meant to play this part?* Lord help me to find a new way to be human. This self-identity thing was killing me softly.

I am not smart. I have a strong accent and I sound weird when I talk. At school, I don't have many friends; nobody wants to sit next to me at lunch table because I was different.

I didn't have great personality, and I was not fun to be around with. It became me against the world. I was not thinking Christ like things because I didn't have the light in me.

After living with the Jackson's family for several months I had my yearly checkup. The doctor notice there was something wrong with me. One of the main concerns was my shortness in structure and I also told him that I was not having menstruations and so they did some special tests. I had no idea what kind of tests they were doing or what was going on but I cooperated and did whatever needed to be done.

December came. We went back to the doctor's office. Now you can only imagine when a person is hearing a bad news from the doctor. "Well I don't know what to say but we did found something from the lab test". "Oh really?" my foster mom said. My heart began pounding as I listened to the sound of his voice. "Doctor, what is it? Please tell me!" My voice trembled. "Well, we're not really sure what it is yet but I think you might have something like turner syndrome." He said. What in the world is that? I've never heard of it before. Maybe it's not so bad. This was the powerful surprise news I'd ever received in my entire life. Before I could even ask the doctor questions, he saw the confusion and devastations in my face. He read my mind.

He did not fully explain it but he gave little of introduction. "I'm not 100% sure what it is and I don't want to give you the wrong information. I'm going to referred to see a specialist. It one of the hospitals located in Denver. It is called the children's hospital. It is one of the best hospitals in Colorado State and I promise you'll be well taken care of. He wrote the doctor's name, phone number and address on a piece of paper. Then he handed it to me.

We walked out the door and into the parking lot. I could see the stunt face on my foster mom's face. Neither of us said a word. It was dead silent the whole time we were in the car driving home.

So we made an appointment and I saw the doctor in Denver. That was when I was diagnosed with turner syndrome. "Turner syndrome is a genetic condition in which a female does not have the usual pair of two X chromosomes." I stared at her with a blink face. "Ok. What does that mean?" I sat there and listened tentatively . . .

I was in 9th grade when I was diagnostic with turner syndrome

I was speechless and really terrified when I was diagnosed with this disease.

I felt like I was being cursed and all I could think of was "why me?" Lord, if you can hear me, please answer. I just want to know.

As the doctor tells me the causes and went through the list of symptoms, I think kind of went numb. I didn't know what to say or how to respond. I stared at her with blink eyes.

As much as I hated this news, as much as I wanted to block it out, I couldn't. This was the hardest truth I couldn't deny or run away from if I try. Why me Lord? Isn't my life already bad enough? What do you want from me God? I'd just moved here this family. I'd just started 9th grade in high school. I thought I was doing well. Can't you just give me a break? These are the things I would say when I'm alone in my room. I would pour out my frustrations and complain to God. Six months later, I had another visit at the Children's Hospital in Denver. I yet got another bad news. I'm truly sorry to tell you this. People with this condition usually are unable to have children. Turner syndrome prevents the ovaries from developing properly, which affects a girl's sexual development and the ability to have children. "Wait! What!? What are you talking about? I'm taking the hormones and the growth injection, shouldn't that help?" "Yes, I agree. But I'm truly sorry. Though these treatments will help you with growth and development, it is not enough. You aren't developing ovaries in order to have children. Look on the bright side. There are many children that need a family. Maybe you can adopt them and give them love."

Shocked and frozen.

I don't like to admit it but I'll go ahead and throw it out there. Overwhelmed at the point this was too much information I can handle. Tears were running down my cheeks like a waterfall. I couldn't stop the tears from falling. I felt incomplete and living in a dry season. Dry lightning flash across the sky but no rain. I was overcome with bitterness in my heart. I was not happy with who I was. For the way God created me.

As a young adult, I knew I wanted to dedicate my life to helping others and making a difference in my community. Growing up in a Christian home, and attending church on a regular basis, help my faith to grow a little more stronger.

Four months before my Eighteen birthday my caseworker told me I was progressing very well and I was mature, responsible and she would consider letting me move out of the foster home. A month later, she spoke with her boss and I was approved to move out. May 2010, was the month I would be moving. I was excited and happy to finally live on my own and try to gain some independent. The day finally came! All my stuff were packed and loaded in the car.

After a couple of month of living on my own, not even a year something tragic happened. It happened all because of my mom; all because of one little decision. My friend and I were in downtown. We sating at the bus station to catch a bus to her house. It was Saturday and we were going to celebrate her neigfew's birthday. I was sating at the chair, the buses were pulling in and I was looking out for the one I was going take when suddenly a woman walked, passed in front of me. That looked familiar and I thought for sure it was my mom. So I called slowed with an uncertain voice. "Mom?" She turns around and looks at me; not recognizing me for a moment. Both our eyes meet and I knew for sure it was my mom! "Mom!?" I was shocked, lost and confused. It was my mom. Can it be? No, I must be dreaming! I got up and give her a hug but I think she was scared and didn't quite recognize me at first. She stood there like a status. And her hands were sniffed to her side. She did not move an inch or give me a hug. I felt like I was hugging a tree. Yet, I was crying tears of joy. "Where are you going?" She asked. "To my friend's house." I grabbed her hand and we walked to the bus. "This is the bus we are taking. Come with us." She got on the bus and we went. I asked my friend to give my mom some rice and chicken. We quickly fed her and after she was done, she wanted to go home." It was Saturday and the buses stop running around 7. She would have to catch two buses in order to get to the apartment. I had completely forgotten about it. So I asked my friend how long the party would be, she said she was going to stay overnight. I needed to somehow take my mom home. I asked if her neigh can give my mom and I a ride home but he said there was a low gas in the car and that they don't have enough money to put gas in the car. I called taxi and told her it would be here within the next thirty minutes. Thirty minutes pass, it didn't show up. She kept nagging I want to go home and take a shower. We kept waiting and waiting, an hour had passed. Finally I called someone and they took us home. She took a shower and I got her some cleaned clothes. I put a blanket on the floor, next to my bed and asked if she wanted to sleep on the bed but she said no and lay on the floor. I got in bed next her bed I couldn't sleep. Is this real? I still couldn't believe my mom was alive and is right there in front of me. I can literally see her! It was morning! For the first time I was awake with my mom. I got up and made some scramble eggs and toast for her. Then we went to church on that Sunday morning. I don't know what but she started complaining about the message the pastor was preaching. I couldn't understand most of what she was saying. She said something about the church being mean, and talking negative about people. I told her and that it has nothing to do with her. She kept nagging and asking me to tell her what they were saying. I try really to ignore her but of course I had missed most of the message. After church we came home and I made rice and chicken. Before she even ate it, she started criticizing me. She said the rice was too watery and did not cook well. All I wanted was to yelled at her but I smiled at her and kept calmed. It was after she ate and dinner was over that she started laying all her problems and telling me what a terrible person I was. I got very emotional and lost control. I walked out of the room. Later, she called me and said. "Obviously, you don't want me here. I will leave if you want to." Today is Sunday and buses don't run on Sundays. Just stay until tomorrow morning than you can leave. But she insisted on leaving. I called my friend and he took her. Said "Here we again. After threes of not seeing you, this is all I get." August of 2011, was the last time I saw my mom. Because of this incident; the encounter with my mom I was forced to go back into foster home.

Meeting my mom again was such a bad idea; a terrible experience. I've prayed for God to keep my mom safe and alive, to let me see her one more time before anything happens. But never once in a million year had I imagined it would be this way. As horrible and selfish as this may sound sometimes I kind of wish I'd never seen my mom. I honestly believe that things would be much easier if we never met again. If we were not together we would bound better and our love would become stronger if were apart and not living under the same roof. This is the hardest truth and it is how I really feel about my mom. I'm just really tire of playing this game. She comes and goes; this is very hard for me. It drives me crazy. I constantly have to wonder where she is and what she is doing. Lord is she eating enough food? Is she healthy or she is still alive?

After I met my mom I fell in a major depression. I've always being depressed but I was not diagnosed until now. I use to believe in life, love, liberty, and the "pursuit of happiness." I no longer have the same feelings like I use to, and even if I had them they probably are not as strong and positive as they were before. I always felt sad and just had a whole bunch of attitudes. My negative attitudes were affecting the people around me. I couldn't make friends and keep them long. I was beautiful on the outside but on the inside I feel disgusted and ugly; nobody really likes that. When I was diagnosed PTSD and was finally able to get help I became a healthier and happier person. I was saved mentally and physically.

When people ask me who I was and whom I came with in America. "No ma'am, no sir I am not here alone. I came with my mom. The next question would almost always be "Where is she?" As uncomfortable this may be, I have to answer with "I don't know." She is somewhere in the state. The last time I heard, she was in so and so location, doing so and so. That's all I know."

So you see, I'm all out of faith and this is how I feel.

About three days later, I was told I had to move to a foster home. I remember specifically being angry and disappointed with myself and upset with my caseworker and the whole thing. There was no warning whatsoever. They told to move out of the apartment. They didn't even give me time to pack or say goodbye to my roommate. I was only giving a time to pack couples of clothes and personal hygiene. Last but not least, I was not introduce to the person I was going to stay with. As scared and angry I was I managed to keep calm. I didn't want to make a bad impression.

Lord, I can't seem to feel my breathe. I can't find the words to speak. I don't feel anything; I am emotionally shouted down. I was completely numb from the pain.

I went through identity crisis. Who am I? Where am I from? Am I African or American person? This was not the life I've imagined. This was not supposed to happen.

I decided to tackle my problems once and end it in the most unimaginable way.

I'm tire of this life. I try to hold unto this world with everything I'd got but I feel the weight of this world, pulling on my shoulders. Lord, I don't know how to get through another day.

I'm tangled up inside and I'm losing my faith. I'm overwhelmed by all the things around me and suddenly I can't help but feeling crazy and going nuts. My heart and soul was broken. Every day was the same just trying to survive. So I said, "I'm done with this life. Here comes another day, here comes another try but I'd rather give it up than give it another chance. So I decided suicide was the only solution to my problems, to my life.

I sat down to write a goodbye letter to the people whom I'd loved. At that time, I was being selfish. I wasn't thinking about anybody else but me. I wasn't thinking about all those people who had loved me and how I was going to hurt them.

My beloved friends,
Please don't cry for me.
It was not my intention
To bring grief in your hearts.
I have suffered for quite a while now,
Let your love make me go in peace and
Embrace in my father's arms.
Do not hold me back. I must go where I've been called.
I don't want to live with a wounded heart
And live my whole life feeling hurt.
The pain is not healthy for our hearts,
Please let me leave in peace.
You are crying now but soon you'll think
and remember all the good times we had together;
There will be joy in your heart. I
want to go to heaven and
I pray soon you too will follow me!
In heaven, there is a new breath of life.
Life below cannot be compared to the one above.
There is no worried. All my pains will be diminished.
In heaven, there is no sorrow; only
laughter and happiness.

After I finished writing, I went to my room and grabbed couple of piles. At that time I had a medicine that was for the fungus on my toes, I was taking birth-control. First, I took two of each prescribed medication. I waited for the like 5 minutes but nothing was working. So I went again and took another two of the fungus medicine. Again, I waited but it didn't work. So I took another two and decided that wasn't enough and I needed something stronger. I went to the kitchen and took four of the Ibuprofen. Then I started to feel a little dizzy and nauseated. I went to into my room lie on the bed and closed my eyes; hopping that I would fall asleep and never wake up again to see another light of the day. But I was wide a weak. "Are you serious? Why can't you just let me die?" I grabbed my phone and text my foster mom. I text, *Please help! With what?* She texted me back. *Overdosed.* I responded. *Overdosed with homework? No.* I text her back. *Overdosed! Are you serious? OK. Just stay there. I will be there as soon as I can. The next thing I know, there were cars and ambulance flashing at the door.*

Ok. I know it was wrong. I let emotions overtake me and I didn't make the wise decisions.

I've never given much thought as how I would die. I've heard of death. In fact I probably know more about death than most people. I've watched people get killed and have seen some buried. I've lose some close friends and family. I never once thought of killing myself; it was not something that ever crossed my mind; but that was a story different during my teen years. Since then it just sort of became a habit and has haunted me ever since then. It was like catching a small fever. It comes and goes whenever it wants and however it wants. One minute I would be fine and the next thing I know I'm feeling sick again.

Sure I have seen and heard on the news and even read many stories about people who had become suicidal or has successfully taking away their own life. There were times I would criticized them and thought it was idiotic. I simply did not understand why they couldn't figure out ways to deal with those issues. But as I look back now and remember those moments, I realize that I was only in denial. I too had problems but was afraid to admit it. I never once imagine falling in the deep pit and wanting to commit suicide.

September of 2012 was the year and the month I've reached my breaking point.

I lost my consciousness and went crazy. I'm only human. I try everything within my power to stay strong and fight to the finish line but I lost my faith. Life has gotten the best of me and I gave it in. My life was in a whole lot of mess and I became suicidal. I thought life was nothing but a fading dream. I was always a good kid and try to live by right. I was a good person who never got in trouble in school and always works hard in school. I never did drugs, alcohol or even smoke. I love life and love being around people; particularly my friends and family. I had wonderfully people in my life. Some of them knew about my issues and everything I was going through. But I always feel like there is a visible wall when I'm going through a stressful time.

I felt like I'm worthless and just don't deserve to live. I wanted to show and let the world know that something was clearly wrong in my life. I wanted so much to believe in love and life but I was haunted by severe depression. It was at this point that I became suicidal.

Lord, what is my purpose? Why am I here on earth if I can't make the best of this life for me? I feel like I'm going through all this pain and suffering for nothing. It seems like life is hitting me in face and I just want to run and hide. Somewhere unknown, where there's only peace and love.

After the ambulance the came and as I was being taken away to the hospital, they made drink some charcoal, at first I refused. That thing was black, thick and it just smell really terrible.

I was like there's no way I'm going to drink this thing. He said, "You have to drink this so that we can the medication out of your system. We don't want anything to happen to you." "No." Well, you drink it now or we gonna have to strip you down and put it down through your throat." So I took a sip, but he kept looking at me so I drank some more. "I'd had enough. I can't drink this thing anymore." "Ok, but you're not done yet. When we get to the hospital, the doctor is gonna want you to finish this whole bottle." We got at the hospital, the nurse came, took my tempt, blood pressure and said that everything was normal. But they had to do blood simple to make sure none of your organs is damaged. The nurse took my blood, while I was waiting for the result, the nurse made me to drink more charcoal. I was coughing, and throwing up. I felt like I was going to pass out. The thing that me scared and made me worried was the fact that I kept waiting for the result, for the doctor to show up and tell me at least something.

Then my caseworker showed up. I looked at her and smiled. "What are you doing here!? It is late, shouldn't you go home and be with your family." "Yeah, you right. But I wanted to come see you." Just like I'd imagined she started asking me questions. But one thing that stood out and I'll always remember from that day was when I asked Ms.Quinda if my foster mom was going to be in trouble she told me no. Though she try to deny it but I knew something was going to happened but I didn't know what. I asked her if she was mad at me she told me no but she was disappointed in me. "Why did you do it? You are a smart young lady." "You've been through a lot and I know that but this was not an option. You are smart person but sometimes you make wrong decisions. I'd seen it several times and this is one of them." She was not angry at me or anything but for her to be honest and tell me how she truly felt just breaks my heart.

Finally the doctor came in. We're been waiting for quite a long time. I was hungry and tire. All I wanted to do was to go home. It's about time! Everything was ok but I was told I couldn't go home. 24 of September, 2012 I was taken to Aspen Pointe, the mental health hospital. I would stay there for 3-7 days. When I got there I really hated that place. I felt like I was in prison. There was no privacy. The beds were not comfortable at all. And don't even get me started on the food. The foods were not the greatest thing in the world. One time during dinner I couple of hair in my food. I threw it out, got another one but there was also hair. Lord knows I was really happy that time because it was my last day and I was going home so it was no big deal if I didn't have any dinner.

I was supposed to stay there for at least three days but got release early, I try my best to be on my best behavior and do everything I could to get out of that place. And it worked! One day later, I went home.

I had favorable wind and everything was going pretty well.

People say that's great for you. You don't seem to care at all what happened. But it was simply not the truth. Obviously, it was clear that nobody understood how severely my pain was. I put a fake smile on my face. I went to school the next day and pretended as if everything was alright. Deep down my soul things were bitter and cold but I didn't give up on hope. As I was going through this rough path, I believe my faith was being tested. This was a moment of hope, a moment of an opportunity as a Christian for me to reevaluate my life and my walk with Christ. My heart was from the terrible seasoning of pain and suffering but I was not about to give up on life, my future. I was determined to stay strong with God and not let the negative stuff affect my life.

During of the sermon, Pastor Brady had once said, "the enemy would love for us to live in fear; yes it will love for us to live in parallelize and looking over our shoulder. But God has the highest power. He is higher above all things." And I believe that the words of God, in Hebrew 13:6, *So we say with confidence, the Lord is my helper; I will not be afraid. What can man do to me?* In the mist of the storm, in the mist of everything that was going on I was tempted be in fear, by worry and cripple by anxiety. I was hopeless in a predicate situation. I was empty handed and in complete brokenness but I was at complete at peace when I remember the promises and the goodness of God. I knelt down at my feet; I prayed pathetically and said

I trust you with my life, my future, with everything I am. I was not concern about tomorrow or anything else. Life is precious so why waste it now. When we got the news, it was as if an earth quake had hit the house. The whole house became a dark place. I watched the other foster girl, foster mom, and her biological daughter walking around with cold, breezy heart. They were far away from peace, love and forgiveness. They all went down the basement and gather in the room. They were mourning deeply as if it was the end of the world. I, on the other hand, decided to go back to my normal routines. I grabbed my math book and sat at the table and started doing g some school work. I was determined to stay strong and not let anything break me down.

As I was doing homework, mind was not completely focused. I thought about my action, what I did and everyone I'd hurt. There was a voice inside my head saying "It was such a stupid thing you did. You are a smart and talented girl, why did you do that kind of thing? You are such a disgrace to this family. You always carry bad lucks with you. Wherever you go, something bad always happen!" I wanted to scream and yell. "No, stop it!" My heart was filled with remorse and sorrowed tears. It felt like there was a volcano growing inside of me and just ready to explode. But I refused to let it show. I went down the basement to check on the rest of the family. I knocked softly on the door and pocked my head in. "Hey guys. How are you all feeling?" They all turned around and looked at me as I stood in front of the door. I saw those reddish eyes, and swollen faces that seems to say "Get out of here now! We don't want anything to do with you.

We do not want to see your face. This is all your fault." The foster mom sniffed and said, "It is hard, you know. And we're all sad about this situation." I took a deep breath and said softly, "Yes, I know very well. And I'm truly sorry." You can come cuddle and cry with us if you would like to." I smile and said, "Ok. Thanks but I'm going to head upstairs and continue studying. I walked away.

It was than that the light came up. I realized than this was a game of "Monkey in the Middle." I was the monkey who was reaching and crying out for help. For the next few weeks before we had to move nobody wanted to talk with me. I try open communication and apologizing, but I was only at a dead end. Finally, I Said to my foster mom, "you know what I'm sorry for what I did but not the way I did it.

Being in a foster home sometimes made me regrets coming to America. Growing up as a child, I thought my country was the best thing in the world. I thought my life in Africa was normal. My family was not poor and I had never experienced the hunger.

Behind Closed Door

THE SUN CRAWLS SLOWLY and disappears behind the little gray clouds, giving way to the darkness of the evening. Once again it is bedtime; the longest and the hardest part of the day. I brush my teeth, took a shower, and put on my pajamas. Then I go to my room and close the door behind me. I knee down at my feet, on the edge of my bed. I bow my head and say a prayer. I go to bed and close my eyes but sleep would not come visit me.

It is dark and quiet. I look up at the ceiling. The reality had kept me awake, haunting me through the night.

It has been three years since I've seen my mom. The last time I saw her was in a court room when the final decision was made and her rights were terminated. I've not spoken to her nor seen her for the past years. It felt almost as if she has disappeared from the face of the earth. *Lord, I pray and ask that you would keep her safe.* I pray the same prayer over and over again. But each year passes and nothing changed. I think about death a lot more since my mom has been gone. I constantly think about her. I wonder where she's at. I wonder what she is doing. Does she have enough food to eat? Does she have clean, warm clothes to wear? And if she was alive, does even think about me? Those were top questions that were constantly pondering in my heads. Each and every day, I pray for more and more hoping that I'll see her again someday. I realize that my love for her keeps growing bigger and stronger every day.

I keep praying and waiting for an answer, a miracle to happen. That's all I can do.

It was late in the evening. As usual, the village seems quite. Some people gather around a campfire. They were telling stories and cracking jokes. All of suddenly, a scream of panic cut through the air. It was a sound of pregnant women, crying out for help. It took a few seconds for me to realize what was going on. Of course during that time, I was young and didn't quite understand what was happening. I thought something horrific had happened to our mom or maybe she was really sick. I never had seen my mother like this before. I could see she was in a great deal of pain. And I had really thought I we were going to lose and never see her again. I was horrified with fears and immediately started crying. My mom was in labor!

I look around, taking in the familiar area of my surroundings. This was my home. A place I once lived in. I must take in every details of every corner. This will have all to remain in my memory and live in my heart.

Not many people get the wonderful opportunity to come to America. When I reflect back at my life it is still astonishing to see how far I've come.

I went to Guinea and saw her, she was pretty much sick. I notice that she had lost a lot of weight but I was extremely overjoyed when I united with her again. We registered refugees and we stayed in the camp for a while and then moved to Ivory Coast. Being in the big city and actually being able to come here was a privilege. It is like taking the act test because it wasn't simple. There are certain things that were required. There was an interview, treatments and tons of paper works. Therefore, there were certain numbers of people that were allowed to come to U.S. Out of all these people my mom and I were one of the blessed ones to come.

I hear a voice, like a fairy Godmother whispering softly to me. "My child, all your hard work has finally paid off. It happened. All your dreams is finally coming true!"

In order to fit in and be like a typical American, my mom decided to change my name.

For she thought my African would be too difficult to pronounce and spell. She then gave me a few choices to let me choose my new name. Back than I could not speak or write well, I wanted something simple. "How about Princess?" She blurred it out.

"Yeah, I kind of like it." I told her.

Princess was a common name for African girls. We decided to go with that one. She gave me few days to study the name and learn how to spell it. I thought it was going to be a piece of cake but it was more difficult than I'd imagine. "How about Levia?" She asked me. Hmm . . . I never heard of that name before but it does sound interesting. "Levia! I like it. It is a rare name with five letters." Then I thought my last name is Gee so it sounded great together-Levia Gee was pretty cool. I looked over it few times and I was able to say it properly as well as spelling it.

I wake every morning and I look out the window. I can see the birds flying high above the trees and I can hear the sweet sound of the birds singing. At the same time, I graciously wonder how there could be such a day. My heart is filled with despair and sorrows and yet the birds sing happily and the air is filled with sweet smells of springs. Someone please tell me, how there could be such a day. How can it even exist when my nightmares are still there?

I'm reaching out to someone in the middle of my breaking dreams. I need to take a deep breath and set my mind straight. Yes I must stay strong

Darkness cannot drive out darkness;

only light can do that.

Hate cannot drive out hate;

only love can do that.

Martin Luther King, Jr.

Forgiving is not forgetting,

It's your precious little angel. I just wanted to stop by and say hi; I also have something to tell you. First let me say I'm doing great and everything is fine. I miss you so much tonight. I am thinking of you and wonder where you are. I hope you're doing well. Your little girl is turning into a strong and beautiful young woman. I wish you could see her now and kiss her good night. She smiles a lot when she thinks about you; but sometimes she gets sad and cries because she loves you so much.

It is really frustrating how when I go about my usual day and suddenly I think about you for no specific reason. That often happens you know. I remember mom and think about you when I'm happy, I remember and think about you when I'm sad. Unfortunately, it breaks my heart because we're strangers. We have never met each other before; I don't know you and you don't know me. All I know is I belong to someone because God created something unique and beautiful as me.

I wish to tell you today is a very special and an important day to me. See I'm graduating today. The moment I've been waiting for is finally here. Yes I'm proud to say I made it all the way. I wish you and mom were here to see me walk across the stage. It took quite a long for me to accomplish this but hey I did it. It was not easy.

Some people had asked me how it feels to graduate from high school. I wish I could tell them it feels great but I can't. I tell them it does not really feel any different because I'm already ahead of the game. I've began taking colleges classes at PPCC. I can only smile and say "I'm officially a college student." I say it loud and proud. I struggled really hard in school. There were times I dropped to my knees and cry; all my strength was gone and there was no fight left in me. I thought the world was a cruel place and I was ready to give up on life. I really didn't like school. It was too difficult for me. I thought doing homework was a torture. Another thing I hated the most was getting up early in the morning. But I didn't want to act bad and get in trouble so I did my best to go to school every day. I think life struck me the most during my junior and senior years of high school. I was placed in a new foster home halfway through my junior year. Then at the beginning of my senior year, they moved me again. I must say this was my 5th home. My 5th home was with Ms. Carrie. I love Ms. Carrie. I think it is the best home I've lived in so far. Not to say it is perfect. We have our issues sometimes but that's normal. She is a single parent and sometimes she gets very emotional and breaks down. It is not pretty. It is almost like the whole world is crushing down when she gets stress out. I hate seeing her like this. Sometimes I get scared. Things happen in every family and every home. Trust me nothing is perfect in this world. At first it was very difficult because it was around Christmas and I was in middle of finals. I was terrified because I was afraid I was going to fail my classes and not graduating on time. I felt like my life was a hell. But I was determined to make to it.

Look dad, please don't be disappointed. I'm not a terrible person. I'm a people pleaser. I try my best to behavior well and to set a good impression. Many people are fooled by the mask I wear but eventually I take it off; sooner or later, they see me. I'm not the person I set out to be. I don't like to hide my true colors. I spend many times analyzing and feeling sorry for myself. I thought I was the most hatful person in the world. I try to remember and understand that not everyone has to love me or even like me.

I'm only human and I make mistakes. Everybody loses control sometimes. I am looking for love out on own. I wanted everybody to like me but I've learned that you can't force love. I've being searching and wandering; times and times again I only get hurt. So the only way to prevent this and to protect myself was to hurt them first before they can hurt me.

I'm not your average spoiled teenager. For the most part, I was a good kid. I went to church almost every Sunday and never once disobey my foster parents. I was not mean or manipulative. I never did drugs or drink alcohols. But for some reason I behaved in a way that hurts people and pushes them away. I never fully open my heart to them. Yes, I was successful in pushing people away. If there was a trophy or prize I probably could have won. Acts of confusions and anger seemed to rule my every move.

Look dad, I'm not telling all this because I have to; I just thought you should know a little more about me. I recently graduate from high school and I'm currently attending Pikes Peak community colleges. When I think I about my life, I can't believe how I've come. I've heard many say teen years are one of the most difficult periods of a person's life I didn't believe it until it happen to me. I'm writing to you because I need someone to talk; someone to open myself to. I want to have a place of my own and finally feel free; but I'm only one step closer.

All my life, I have worked for a change;
Today I will make my dream come true
I hope to make the world a better place

A Note To God

LORD, I LIFT MY hands. I give you glory and honor for who you are and not because of your unfailing love you've shown me. You are my rock and salvation. Each and every day you grant me strengths to stand firm against the enemy. Thank you Lord for holding me so securely as I walk through this world.

The reality was things are always harsh. It does not matter who you are or where you come from.

I don't laugh or smile as much as I used to

Rejections, pain and suffering is all I've ever known my entire life. Now I know what you're probably thinking; who hasn't experience any pain in their life? Well, let me tell you this, my life has mainly revolved around momentous of unforeseen events and crisis. Through it all, all I wanted was to be accepted. I need someone to come grab my hands and walk with me along the beach. I needed someone to come and whisper to me, that sweet sound to tell me I was loved and that everything would be alright. But every day, I feel like a plastic bag drifting away through the wind. When I'm blown away by the wind, no one is able to catch me. I sometimes feel like an invisible wall; no one notice me when I walk by.

There are days when I feel great and happy. It seems like everything was stable and moving forward as planed but then there are days when certainly everything comes back. I have to
remember the past and relive the horrible memories.

I was one of Whitney Houston's biggest fans. She was my idol; not that I worship her or anything but she sure was one of my favorite greatest singer of all time, sadly this led to distraction and took away her life. She was such an inspiration to me. Sometimes when I compare my life to hers, I thought mine was saddest and the worst thing in the world. I mean she had everything: a family, a big house. She also was rich and everybody loved her. I think "man! This is the kind of life I want." But I guess it was one of those wild dreams a person can only have. Of course I didn't mean it. I didn't really want her life. It was all just a dream; my imagination. What I didn't realize was even the richest and the famous people like Michael Jackson, Whitney Houston; they all struggle with life like the rest of us. Whitney had a dark side and so did Michael Jackson. She was using drugs which led to her death. Now I think I don't want that to happen to me too. Life is precious for it to be waste.

I can't deny that I was tempted many times, on several occasions. There were times I felt like life was getting the best of me. I wanted to be a party girl, go out and drink with my friends. Yes and do drugs and forget all about life. But I knew that was not what life was about. So I made a vow to myself. No matter what happens, I will never drink or do drugs.

If there is one lesson I learned through all these experience, through all these storms is that I'm not guarantee to have a marvelous life but I'm guarantee that God will provide sources and carry me through the dark age; that I may try to live a better life.

Eight years ago if someone would have come to me and speak to me about the idea and concept of spirituality and religious I would look at them with a cold, stone face and simply just laugh. If there is such thing as God or something bigger than ourselves, than why are we going through the pains and suffering? I would argue that my life was perfectly fine and that I did not any awaking or someone to direct my life. But now I have different perspectives on life.

I've completely changed. I'm not the same old girl I once was. My fear was always if I don't act right, they will kick me out; I will have to move again.

Spirituality came in my life shortly after my mom and I moved here. When we first came, mom was connected with some groups and people from church. Many communities from the church helped us a lot. On most Sundays, some people offered us a ride to church. Though we attended church, I really could read the scripture or speak the language well but I think I kind of went along with the whole thing because I was supported my mom. We were getting a lot of help and so I felt like this was the only I could show appreciation and give back to the community.

I think the whole spirituality and religion thing we became sharper and clearer to me as I became more adapted to the culture. I went to school and I started to read and speak English better. This gave me more confidence. I was actually able to pick up the Bible, read it on my own and it made sense to me. Another thing that also helped influence my religious beliefs was when I was place in a foster home. My first foster home was a Christina home and we attended church on most Sundays. Also, as I grew older I had more access to church. I had more selective choice to different churches.

In the process of making sense of the world for myself, I dramatically changed from the alternative to the traditional paradigm. It was like an old song calling my new name.

I switch gear to more of the postmodernism. I begin to question the authority of the church and tried to wonder why they believe in God and how they know if He even exists. I think I became more interested as I attended church and begin to observe their behaviors and the environment of the church. It was than I've gain sense of morality, I now can easily tell differences between good and bad. I especially despise it when other curse around me. I'm trying to gain a better of the world and unit with God as one.